Arata
THE LEGEND

21

We are Man, born of Heaven and Earth,
Moon and Sun and everything under them.

Eyes, Ears, Nose, Tongue, Body, Mind...

Purity will pierce evil and
open up the world of darkness.

All life will be reborn and invigorated.

Appear now.

3 1336 09794 8658

STORY & ART BY
Yuu Watase

Arata
THE LEGEND

CHARACTERS

KOTOHA

A young maiden of the Uneme Clan who serves Arata of the Hime Clan. Possesses the mysterious power to heal wounds.

MIKUSA

Swordswoman of the Hime Clan. Although she is an Uneme, she cannot use the power of the Amatsuriki. Is this because she, like Hinohara, came from the modern world...?!

NASAKE

Although Zokusho of Ameeno, one of the Six Sho, Nasake travels with Arata.

ARATA HINOHARA

A kindhearted high school student who wanders into Amawakuni from the modern world. He is entrusted with the Hayagami Tsukuyo, as well as the fate of the world.

The Story Thus Far

Arata Hinohara, finding himself in Amawakuni, a land in another dimension, is chosen as the successor to the legendary Hayagami Tsukuyo. In order to stop the fighting that ensued after Princess Kikuri's collapse, he continues his journey to make all the Sho submit and unify the Hayagami.

Nasake, the Zokusho of Ameeno, one of the Six Sho, appears before Arata and wishes to submit. Accepting Nasake's offer to guide them to Ameeno's domain, Arata and company board a ship. But the ship is wrecked on the shore of an uninhabited island ruled by Ikisu, another of the Six Sho.

Ikisu, meanwhile, has been pursuing Arata. Appearing suddenly on Kadowaki's airship, Ikisu uses his scent Kamui to bewitch Kanate and snatch him away.

21 Arata THE LEGEND

CONTENTS

CHAPTER 198
Hostility 5

CHAPTER 199
One's Intentions 23

CHAPTER 200
Scream 41

CHAPTER 201
Dash 59

CHAPTER 202
Wind 77

CHAPTER 203
Loss 99

CHAPTER 204
Rampage 117

CHAPTER 205
Must Stop Him 135

CHAPTER 206
Shock 153

CHAPTER 207
To the City 171

Chapter 198

HOSTILITY

IKISU OF THE SIX SHO HAS THE KAMUI OF SMELL.
COULD IKISU BE ON THIS ISLAND?!
YATAKA! I'VE BEEN WANTING TO BEAT SOME SENSE INTO YOU!
WOOSH
THE FEELING IS MUTUAL, KANNAGI!
YOUR IN-SOLENCE IS UNFORGIVABLE !

HOMURA!
ZEKUU!
THOOM
?!

SAIKUUHA!
OKORO!
FWOOSH
STOLEN DANRYU!

KA-BOOM
FIRE?

BOOM
WHAT WAS THAT SOUND?

THAT'S NOT... WELL, IT IS POS-SIBLE.
He was in a bad mood.
SEEMS LIKE IT...
IS KANNAGI ON A RAMPAGE?

KRUNCH

WHAT IF IKISU...
LET'S GO, YOU GUYS!

WOOO
SHEEN
KOTOHA!
SHUDDER
POP
...
WHAT'S WRONG?

I'M SO TIRED ...
I CAN HARDLY MOVE.
?
I'M... NOT COMING.
MIKUSA!
ZOOM
NASAKE?

HE'D JUST IGNORE US ANYWAY.
WOULD YOU MIND GOING ALONE, ARATA?
...
MIKUSA! C'MON!
WE HAVE TO GET TO KANNAGI.
BOOM
WHAT'S WRONG WITH YOU GUYS ALL OF A SUDDEN?
NASAKE ?
I'D BE NO HELP EITHER.
...
I'LL WAIT HERE.
ALL RIGHT THEN! STAY HERE!

BOOM
BOOM
GRAAH!
FWOO
OO
SWIP

FWOO SH
?
HAM
OW!
WHAT ARE THOSE TWO DOING?
KANNAGI! YATAKA!

STOP! STOP IT!
HEY, YOU TWO! CUT IT OUT!
SHUT UP, ARATA!
WOOSH
WHOA!

KRASH
WE NEED THEM BOTH!
WE'LL SEE WHO'S BETTER, MY HOMURA OR HIS ZEKUU!
I'M SETTLING THINGS ONCE AND FOR ALL WITH THIS GUY!
WHAT? SUBMISSION?
WE *WILL* SETTLE IT, KANNAGI. AND YOU'RE GOING TO SUBMIT TO ME!
SHUT UP, ARATA!

TSUKUYO!
KA-BOOM
NOW... HOW TO STOP THOSE TWO...
UMM ...
APPEAR!
NAKISAWA!
YOU TWO...

SPLOOSH
COOL IT!
HAS THAT KNOCKED SOME SENSE BACK INTO YOU?
...

KRK
OH...
FSSS
HOMU-RA!
WOO
ZEKUU!
HEY!

KRAK
WHAM
!

IS
SUAL
EED.
THOSE TWO HAVE FOUGHT MANY TIMES, THOUGH NEVER FOR SUBMISSION.
WHAT...
WHAT'S WITH YOU GUYS?
ARATA...
SMELL?
I DON'T SMELL ANY-
SNIFF
IF WATER DIDN'T DILUTE IT, THEN YOU MUST FIND ITS SOURCE.
YORUNAMI!
IF IKISU'S KAMUI USES SCENT, COULD IT BE MANI-PULATING THEM?
DO YOU SMELL ANY-THING?
EVERYONE'S ACTING WEIRD!
IKISU, WHERE ARE YOU?
Ah!
DON'T TELL ME KOTOHA AND THE OTHERS ...

...ARATA.
THIS WAS MY DOING ...
IT'S NOT IKISU.
WHUP
WHUP
KANATE!

CHAPTER 199
ONE'S INTENTIONS

HEY, ARATA.
KANATE!
!

KNOCK
ZEKUU!
HOMURA!
KANNAGI! YATAKA! STOP FIGHTING!
LOOK, IT'S USELESS.
INSIDE THIS SPHERE...
...IS A SCENT THAT CONTROLS EMOTIONS.
I SMASHED TWO OF THEM IN THE WIND.
ONE, "ANGER," I SENT TOWARDS KANNAGI AND YATAKA.
THEY GOT A WHIFF OF IT AND NOW THEIR FURY WON'T ABATE.

THE OTHER WAS "LETHARGY."
IT MADE KOTOHA AND THE OTHERS LISTLESS.
ANGER AND LETHARGY?
THE KAMUI OF SMELL BELONGS TO IKISU, ONE OF THE SIX SHO...
KANATE! WHY DID YOU...
IT'S SIMPLE, ARATA...
SO I COULD FIGHT YOU!

KANATE, THIS ISN'T...
HAPPUJIN...
!

SHIK
ERG!
SHIK
NIGANA!
SHIK
KUGURA!
AWAKEN SHINADO! FIGHT HIM WITH WIND!
ARATA! HIS HAYAGAMI ORIGINALLY CAME FROM SHINADO!
TMP
UNH...

FIGHT HIM?
HOW CAN I...
...FIGHT KANATE?
HUH?
BAM
BAM
YOU HAVE TO DEFEAT ME TO FREE KOTOHA AND THE OTHERS!
WHAT ARE YOU WAITING FOR, ARATA?

THIS SCENT BALL WILL NEUTRALIZE WHAT THEY SMELLED!
ONLY I CAN SHATTER IT.
IF YOU DON'T DEFEAT ME, THEY'LL STAY AS THEY ARE NOW!
!
UP
KANATE, WHAT'S HAPPENED TO YOU?
THIS ISN'T YOU.
YOU WOULDN'T DO SOME-THING LIKE THIS.
KRA
QUIT YAKKING!
I WANT...
NG

...TO BE THE SHO THAT MAKES YOU SUBMIT!
AH!
WHAT'S THIS?
TUG TUG
THERE'S A SMELL... ON KANATE.
IS KANATE IS BEING CON-TROLLED BY IKISU?!
NIGANA!

ENOUGH...
IKISU, WHERE ARE YOU?
...ARATA HINOHARA? I'M RIGHT HERE.
DID YOU CALL ME...

GACK
DID HE THINK HE COULD ENTER MY TERRITORY UNDETECTED?
AS FOR THE CAPITAL AND THE OTHER DOMAINS...
I SMELL EVERY-THING.
THIS LAND, THE PEOPLE... EVERY SMELL IS UNDER MY CONTROL.
I, MACHIRUDO, CANNOT STAND THE STENCH OF HUMANS!
AMAWAKUNI AND THAT OTHER WORLD ARE THE SAME!
...THEY STINK! IT'S HORRIBLE.

CALM DOWN, MACHI-RUDO.
I WILL DESTROY THIS WORLD AND ITS PUTRIDITY FOR YOU.
THAT'S WHY I MUST CRUSH ARATA...
THAT GENTLE BOY CAN'T BRING HIMSELF TO FIGHT HIS FRIENDS.
Tee hee ...
THE FASTEST WAY TO DEFEAT SUCH A YOUTH IS TO CRUSH HIS SPIRIT.
KANATE!

!BU
HOMURA!
YATA-KA!
KANNAGI ...
YOU GIVE UP! STOP RUNNING AWAY FROM MY MIRROR OF UTSUBO AND ADMIT DEFEAT.
YATAKA! GIVE UP AND SUBMIT TO ME!
SPLASH

CHIKKA
KYU!
KYU!
KYU
TUP
I'M TOO TIRED.
CHIKKA
CHIKKA
CHIKKA
I DON'T CARE.
MIKUSA... THAT INSECT IS POISON-OUS.
WE SHOULD MOVE...
REALLY?

KANATE!
WAKE UP!
ARATA! USE SHINADO! THAT WILL...
...STOP HAP-PUJIN!
THEN WHAT? MAKE KANATE SUBMIT?
YOU WANT TO TURN EVERYONE BACK TO NORMAL OR DON'T YOU?

HAPPUJIN!
WHY...
...WON'T YOU FIGHT ME FOR REAL?
UNH...

...I BECAME A SHO.
YOU DON'T KNOW THE REAL REASON ...
I'M NOT.
AND I WAS JUST A LOWLY EX-BANDIT, Y'KNOW?
I GUESS YOU COULDN'T. FROM THE TIME I MET YOU, YOU WERE "THE CHOSEN ONE."
KANATE, I NEVER THOUGHT OF YOU THAT WAY!
KRK
ARATA?
DO YOU THINK I'M BEING MANIPULATED?
YOU DON'T UNDER-STAND...

AND AFTER ALL THIS TIME, I STILL HAVEN'T CAUGHT UP.
...HOW SOMEONE LIKE ME FEELS, SOMEONE WHO'S BEEN SCORNED BY SOCIETY AND HIS FAMILY!
YOU DON'T KNOW HOW SICK I AM OF ALWAYS HAVING TO LOOK UP TO YOU!
HEE HEE HEE
KANATE, NO SCENT SUITS ARATA LIKE THIS ONE.
RETSUKA ...

Chapter 200

SCREAM

ARATA!
YOU WERE CHOSEN BY PRINCESS HIME AND BY TSUKUYO.
YOU'LL NEVER UNDER-STAND HOW I FEEL!
IF I WERE STRONG LIKE YOU AND LORD KANNAGI...
IF I WERE A SHO...
WHAK

...AND TRAVELED TOGETHER?
EVEN AFTER WE ESCAPED FROM GATOYA ...
... HOW YOU FELT?
IS THAT ...
YOU REALLY ARE AN AMAZING GUY!
EVEN AFTER THE JOKES AND THE LAUGHS?
ARATA!

WAS IT...
...ALL IN MY HEAD?
I THOUGHT WE WERE FRIENDS ...

ANSWER ME.
KANATE ...

...
ARATA IS AT HIS LOWEST EBB THANKS TO MY "INFERIORITY COMPLEX" SCENT...
WELL, KANATE?
FN
NOUGA!
OOF

YOU'VE ALWAYS LOOKED DOWN ON ME FROM ON HIGH!
HOW COULD WE EVER BE FRIENDS?
SHUDDER
...
FRIENDS?
HA HA HA HA HA...
KLAP KLAP
THIS WILL ROB ARATA HINO-HARA OF HIS WILL TO FIGHT!
THIS IS WONDERFUL! ABSOLUTELY SPLENDID!

YEAH!
JUST LIKE LORD KANNAGI AND LORD YATAKA!
YOU THINK SO?
SURE, THEY MAY HAVE PRETENDED TO JOIN YOUR CAUSE ...
...BUT THEY'RE ONLY INTERESTED IN SUBMISSION!
KLANG
THEY HAVEN'T LISTENED TO A WORD YOU'VE SAID!

CHIKKA
CHIKKA
THEY CAN HEAR THE FIGHTING, BUT WHERE ARE THEY?
IT'S THE SAME WITH THE OTHERS!
ARATA ...
WE HAVE...
...TO MOVE...
POISON-OUS INSECTS ...
CHIKKA
YOU WANT TO FIGHT?
IF YOU STILL WANT TO CHANGE THEM BACK, FIGHT ME.
THEY MAY BE UNDER THE POWER OF SCENT, BUT THAT'S HOW THEY REALLY FEEL!

IS BECOMING STRONG ...
...ALL THAT MATTERS TO YOU?
YES.
IT IS!!

THWUD
GRR

THMP
UNH ...
AGH!
TUG
WHAP
I AM SO DISAP-POINTED ...
...IN YOU.
ARATA?

THE KANATE I KNEW...
...WASN'T WEAK!

...
ARA--

YOU STUPID ...
... FOOL!

FLASH
MY SCENT KAMUI!
ARATA ...
I'M NOT...
KANATE ...
...FIND ARATA ...
WE HAVE TO...
SWAY
SW
AK

WHY?
WHY DOES EVERY-ONE...
OH...
SFF
ARATA ...
ALL THIS TIME...
I GET IT.
ARATA...
I JUST...
...WANTED YOUR APPROVAL.

Chapter 201

DASH

I'M SORRY...
...ARATA.
KANATE ...
YOU'VE COME TO YOUR SENSES.
YOU WERE UNDER THE CONTROL OF IKISU.
...
TMP
I'LL...
...RELEASE YOUR FRIENDS FROM THE SCENT.
HOOM

PO
P
ACK!
KOTOHA!
WHAT ABOUT NASAKE?
MIKUSA! I FEEL SO MUCH BETTER!
OH!

SWOOO

SAME HERE. WHAT I DID WAS...

I JUST WANT TO SAY THAT I HAVE NOTHING AGAINST YOU.

...

NOW I KNOW I'M STRONGER.

TMP
KANATE!
ARATA, TELL KOTOHA AND THE OTHERS I'M SORRY.
...
YOU'RE... GOING BACK TO KADOWAKI?
...SETTLE THINGS...
YES. I'M GONNA ...
...MY WAY.

SETTLE THINGS? WHAT THINGS?
WELL...
WHAT YOU ASKED BACK THERE ...
I THOUGHT WE WERE FRIENDS. WAS IT ALL IN MY HEAD?
YOU'RE...
...REALLY AMAZING.
I'M GLAD YOU VALUE ...
...FRIEND-SHIP MORE THAN STRENGTH. IT MEANS THERE'S HOPE.

HAPPUJIN ...
RRRING
WHOA! WAIT!
WRRRRR
WAIT, KANATE!

...KANATE!
DON'T GO...
TMP
KANATE!
I HOPE...
...HE'S NOT PLANNING TO FIGHT IKISU.
ARATA! I'M SURE THAT'S THE HEART OF IKISU'S DOMAIN!

FWUP
APPEAR!
SHINADO!
ARATA!
!
WOOH
AK
ARATA!
SHINA-DO FAILED.
SPLASH
FWF
UGH...

STRONGER THAN BEFORE!
A MIASMIC WALL...
TMP
IT'S TRYING TO STOP ME!
GAAN
DEMONIC MIASMA?
SPLASH
YES, BUT WE CAN'T TAKE IT RIGHT NOW! THE TIDE IS RISING!
A CAUSEWAY! TO THE MAINLAND!

AND I HAVEN'T BEEN TRAINING. I'D NEED SEVEN MINUTES AT LEAST.
WE WON'T MAKE IT TO THE OTHER SIDE IN TIME. WE'D DROWN WITHOUT THE HELP OF OUR KAMUI!
IT'S ABOUT 3,000 METERS ...
MY FASTEST TIME IN THE 100 METERS WAS 10.37 SECONDS.
BUT THAT WAS A SHORT SPRINT. I'VE ONLY RUN LONG-DISTANCE A FEW TIMES AT CAMP.
I'M GONNA TRY!
HERE I GO!

THE CITY...
SHOO
WAIT, KANATE!
COMPARED TO HIM, I'M...
I WANT TO BECOME STRONG!
I WASN'T BEING MANIPULATED.
I THINK HE KNEW THAT.
YET HE DIDN'T TURN HIS BACK ON ME.
IKISU'S KAMUI JUST EXAGGERATED THE INFERIORITY I FELT TOWARDS ARATA.

I CAN'T EVEN AVENGE MY BROTHER.
HEH...
YOU'LL NEVER REACH ARATA'S LEVEL AND FIGHT FOR OTHERS.
THAT'S THE KIND OF BOY YOU ARE, KANATE.

BIIII

AAGH...
WHAM
IKISU...
SH
WA
K

ENOUGH OF THIS NONSENSE ABOUT FRIEND-SHIP...
...YOU USE-LESS FOOL!

GRR...
SHAKE
I EXPECTED YOU TO HAVE MORE BACKBONE.
OH, KANATE ...
KRK
ARATA...
I WILL MAKE YOU SUBMIT!
I'VE NO USE FOR INCOMPETENT FOOLS.
TMP

GRAAAH!
DON'T DO ANYTHING STUPID!
KANATE!

Chapter 202 WIND
HOLD ON, KANATE!
SOME-ONE'S RUNNING THROUGH THE WATER. IS THAT...
TMP
ARATA?!

Chapter 202
WIND

Arata
THE LEGEND

WHAP
WAIT, YATAKA! LOOK AT HIM GO!
THAT... THAT'S RECKLESS!
HE JUST MIGHT REACH THE OTHER SIDE IN TIME.
SPLAP
SPLASH SPLASH
TRUST ARATA. HE WON'T DROWN. BUT WE'D BETTER FIND A BOAT AND FOLLOW HIM!
RIGHT!
GW
YES, BOTH OF MY KAMUI...
...ARE BEING SUPPRESSED BY THE MIASMA.
SO IS OKORO USELESS TOO?

NO!
ARATA!
SPLASH SPLASH SPLASH
MIKUSA, KOTOHA, LOOK!
THOSE ARE CARNIVOROUS KODAIGYO! IF THE TIDE TAKES ARATA, THEY'LL EAT HIM!
WATER'S RISING FAST!
MAYBE I SHOULDN'T HAVE TRIED THIS!

KANATE!
...GET TO...
I HAVE TO...
HA HA HA HA HA!
TMP TMP
TMP
RAAAH!

SAD TO SAY, NOT EVEN THE KAMUI OF WIND WILL WORK IN MY DOMAIN.
SHAKE
KOOF
COME NOW, KANATE...
THAT WASN'T EVEN CLOSE.
HUFF
AND YOU, IKISU? WHY AREN'T YOU USING YOUR HAYAGAMI?
HA!
WITH TRASH LIKE YOU...
...I LIKE TO AMUSE MYSELF FIRST!
HUFF
WHY NOT MAKE ME SUBMIT BY SMELL?
HUFF
I'VE GOT A FRIEND WHO BELIEVES IN ME...
WELL, I DO.
HUFF
YOU DON'T HAVE ANY FRIENDS, DO YOU!
ANOTHER PERSON-ALITY? MAKE UP YOUR MIND!

HE ALLOWS EMPATHY TO OVERCOME HIS ANGER. THAT IS HIS WEAKNESS!
ARATA HINOHARA COULDN'T BRING HIMSELF TO FIGHT KADOWAKI!
THUN
FRIEND?
AM
FRIEND?
SPLASH
SPLASH
SPLASH
HE WILL NEVER UNITE THE HAYAGAMI!
HE'S A NAÏVE CHILD.
DO YOU UNDER-STAND?
NOW RECITE THE OATH AND SUBMIT TO ME!

UNH...
KADOWAKI ?!

KLANK
HMPH!
HEY, KANATE!
IKISU! ANY BATTLE OF SUBMISSION WILL HAVE TO BE WITH ME!
SO THIS IS WHAT YOU'VE BEEN UP TO SINCE YOU SMASHED MY SHIP.

THIS IS THE HAYAGAMI OROCHI.
IT WON'T ALLOW YOU TO SUPPRESS IT SO EASILY!
AND YOU SHOULD KNOW, SINCE YOU SIX SHO...
...ARE THE ONES WHO GAVE IT TO ME.
FLOOF
NOUGA!
KO
OSH
!
WHAT'S THAT GROSS SMELL?
ARE YOU SOME KIND OF SKUNK?
WEFT
WEFT
WOOSH
GONE ?!
...

KADO-WAKI ...
WHAT ARE YOU... ... DOING HERE?
GEEZ ...
GO BACK TO THE SHIP AND HAVE THEM PATCH YOU UP.
HUH?
I'M LOOKING FOR HIM. I'D FORGOTTEN ALL ABOUT YOU.
I FOUGHT ARATA.
HEH
AND? WHAT HAPPENED TO HIM?
I WENT AT HIM WITH EVERY-THING I HAD.
I GOT TO FIGHT HIM FOR THE FIRST TIME.

PROBABLY ...
G--
SPLA

WHOO M
GO!
PROB-ABLY WHAT?
KADO-WAKI ...
IT'S EASY TO GET ARATA TO FIGHT. HE FIGHTS...
...FOR THE SAKE OF OTHERS.
...
SO...
...FROM NOW ON, KADO-WAKI...
...HE'S ALL YOURS.

TO THE EXALTED SHO...
HAYAGAMI HAPPUJIN NIGANA...

KADOWAKI, YOU'RE STRONG ENOUGH TO GO HEAD TO HEAD WITH ARATA.
YOU CAN DO...WHAT I COULD NOT.
KANATE...
MY SOUL...
...FOR THE SAKE OF YOUR DESTINY...
AND ARATA...
...GET STRONGER.
THIS IS ALL I CAN DO FOR YOU.
YOU...
...I SUBMIT ...

HUFF
HUFF
KANATE!
ARATA...
HINO-HARA?
I KNEW YOU'D COME.
I BELIEVE IN YOU...
...ARATA.
KANATE!

WUSH
THE WIND...
BRO...
GINCHI...
KLAK
GINCHI?
BRO ...
BRO, YOU'RE HERE!
I HEARD BRO'S VOICE!
GINCHI!

WHY...
KRNCH
KADO-WAKI ...
DID YOU...
WHY?
DID YOU? KADO-WAKI...
...MAKE KANATE SUBMIT?
KADOWAKI!
ANSWER ME!

YES.
I MADE HIM ...
...SUBMIT.
LISTEN, ARATA...
THIS IS ALL I CAN DO... AS YOUR FRIEND.

Chapter 203
LOSS

SPLASH
DID YOU...
...REALLY DO THAT?
I...
YES...
...MADE KANATE SUBMIT!
HINOHARA!
ARATA...
BA
BUMP

BA-BUMP
BA-BUMP

BA-BUMP
KANATE ...

BA-BUMP

NOW THAT HE'S INSIDE MY OROCHI...
GRR...
GRAAA!

HN
AM

KADOWAKI!
KWAM
WHY...
...DID YOU DO THAT?
I'M GLAD YOU VALUE...

IT MEANS THERE'S HOPE.
...FRIEND-SHIP MORE THAN STRENGTH.
WHY DID YOU DO IT?!
KADO-WAKI!
KADOWAKI...
...HE'S ALL YOURS.
SO FROM NOW ON...
IT'S EASY TO GET ARATA TO FIGHT.
HE FIGHTS FOR THE SAKE OF OTHERS.

HE GAVE HIMSELF TO ME.
KANATE...
KLANG
SWUP
HAH!
QUIT WHINING!
YOU'RE SUCH A WIMP!

IT WAS A BATTLE OF SUB-MISSION!
THE KID WAS STUPID AND LOST. WHY SHOULDN'T I HAVE TAKEN HIM?
IF YOU'RE UPSET, MAKE ME SUBMIT WITH TSU-KUYO!
BA-BUMP
THEN YOU CAN REUNITE WITH YOUR FRIEND!
BABUMP
KANATE!
BABUMP
THROB
THROB

ドカ
ッ

GRO
06
!
THAT'S ...
?

WHIP
LOOK, KANNAGI!
THAT HUGE DEMON MIASMA ...
I KNOW! BUT HELP ME OUT HERE!
THESE KODAIGYO ARE IN THE WAY!
AND I'LL LEAVE THEM TO YOU.
DO YOUR SHARE!
WHAK
MIKUSA, IT'S DANGER-OUS! GO INSIDE!
THEY'RE NOT USUALLY IN THIS AREA. IT MUST BE THE MIASMA.

KOTOHA!
NO WAY...
ARATA COULDN'T HAVE!
...
CHAK
HE DEMON-IZED.
KRURK
THE WOUND STILL THROBS!
I MAY HAVE PUSHED HIM TOO FAR.
GIVE KANATE...

...BACK!
AWK
HU
TSSHK
Whew!
HE'S FAST!
WH
AH

!!!
G
SHENK

KRK
KRK
KRK
KRK
OROCHI ...
...CAN'T COUNTER ...

FW OOF
HUH?
HA HA HA...
IS THE ALMIGHTY OROCHI ON THE VERGE OF DEFEAT?
LET'S MAKE THIS MORE INTERESTING.
APPEAR ...
SHE
EN
NOUGA!

IKISU!
WHAT SCENT DID YOU USE ON HINO-HARA?
HEH
NOW...
...THERE WILL BE NO STOPPING THAT DEAR BOY.
ZANG

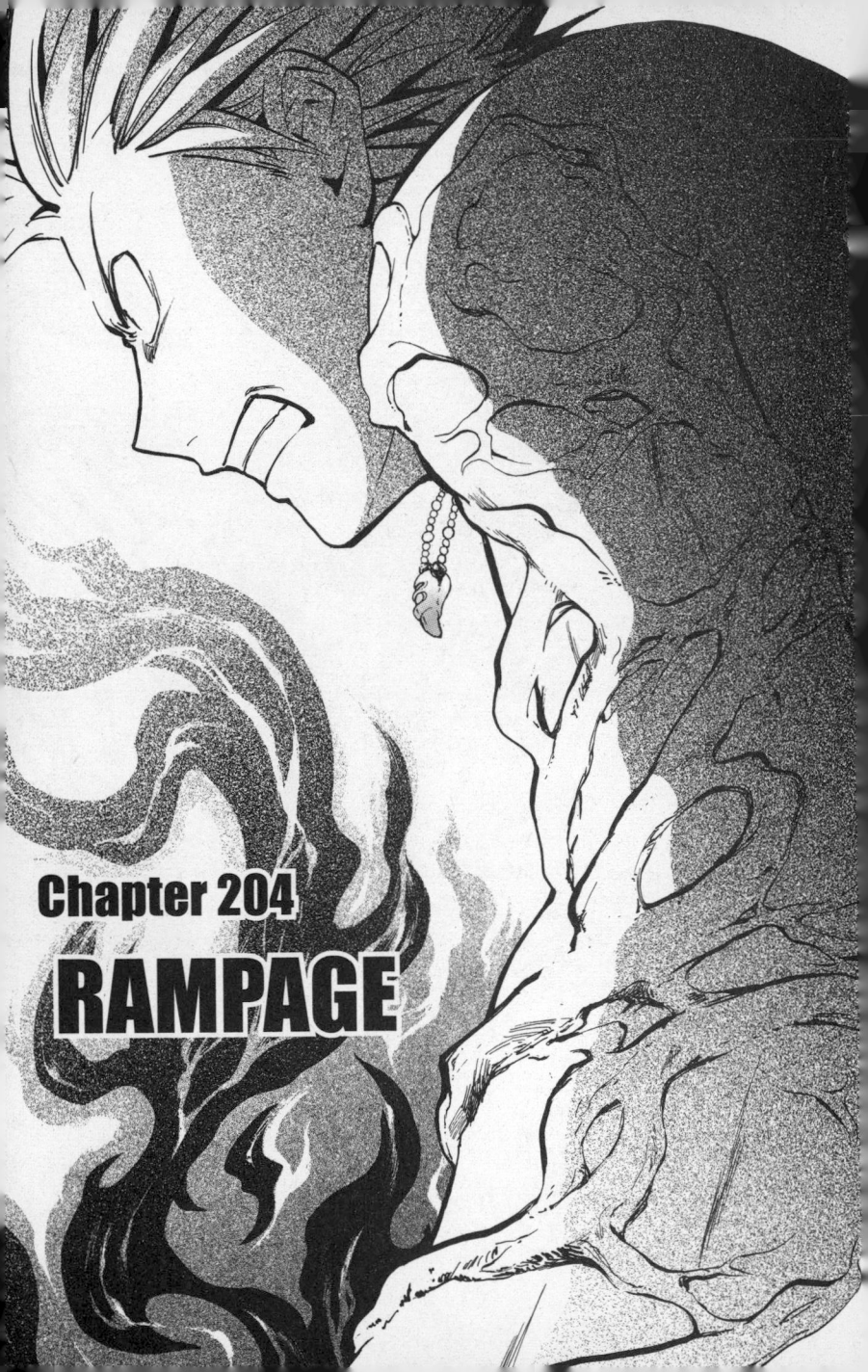

Chapter 204
RAMPAGE

GW
HINO-HARA!
IKISU!
...HIS DEMONI-ZATION WILL BE PERMA-NENT.
ONCE HE INHALES THE SCENT ...

KADO-WAKI!
HA HA HA!
THEN HOW EFFEC-TIVE WILL OROCHI BE?
FW OO
IKISU! STOP!
GIVE KANATE BACK!
KANATE ...
...HE'S ALL YOURS.
SHIK
SHIK
SO FROM NOW ON...

ZAKURO!
SHA
SH
TUMP

WOOSH
SHLOOP
GRAKK

MELOUZAN!

KROOM
RMMMMM
?
THAT'S...
...ARATA!

KSH
GRAAH!
AK
SHRSH
HINO-HARA...
DON'T FALL FOR IKISU'S TRICK!
SHRIP
UNH ...
OOF

KROOS
WHUP
?
HIA

PHEW
THAT SHO ARATA...IS INCREDIBLE!
MUNA-KATA?
WHAT'RE YOU DOING? LET ME GO!
AS YOUR ZOKUSHO, I CANNOT.
YOUR WOUNDS HAVE RE-OPENED.
!
IT'S NOT A FAIR FIGHT. OR DO YOU WANT TO FIGHT SOMEONE...
...WHO DOESN'T EVEN KNOW WHO HE IS ANYMORE?
WE SHOULD LEAVE WHILE WE HAVE THE CHANCE!
KATSU

GRAAA!
LUG
BLUG
BLUG
WORG
WORG
WORG
WORG
RE-TURN ...
... KANATE ...
KADO-WAKI...
HOW MANY TIMES ...
...WILL YOU BETRAY ME?
GLORP
GLORP

SPLASH
LORD MUNAKATA! KADOWAKI?
MISEBI, GET DOWN!
GRUUG
AAAAH!

I'LL MAKE YOU...
...SUBMIT!
THROB THROB
TMP

ARATA!
DID YOU DEMONIZE?
IF SO, SNAP OUT OF IT!
ARATA!
AH...
SHUDDER
WHAT HAPPENED TO KANATE?

SWA
SH
AGH!
YOU'RE NOT A DEMON!
TMP
NO
SH
GEEZ, ARATA!
GET A GRIP!
THAT'S ...
... ARATA?
...

AGH!

SNIP
TING
!
10
MP
HINO-HARA!
KADOWAKI, RUN!

...I CAN STILL EASILY CONTROL HIM WITH SCENT.
IF HE STAYS THIS WAY...
HA HA HA ...
AND IF KADOWAKI DEFEATS HIM, HIS DEATH IS CERTAIN.
HIS MADNESS WILL NOT SUBSIDE UNTIL HE'S MADE YOU SUBMIT, KADOWAKI.
"SADNESS" IS THE SCENT I USED ON HIM!

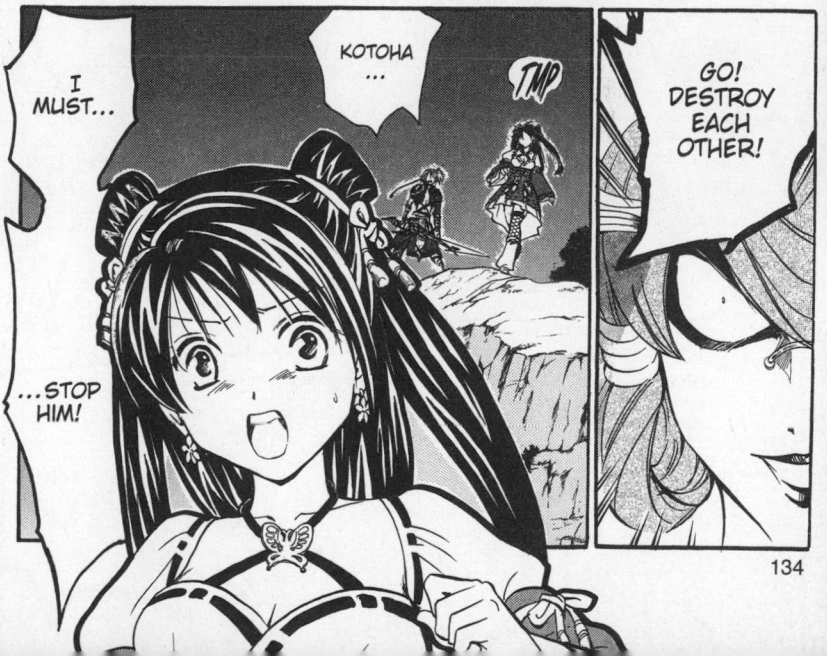
I MUST...
...STOP HIM!
KOTOHA ...
TMP
GO! DESTROY EACH OTHER!

Chapter 205

MUST STOP HIM

I MUST STOP ARATA!
IF HIS DEMONI-ZATION CONTIN-UES ...
NO, NO, I MUST...
THEY'RE RIGHT, KOTOHA. STAY HERE.
IKISU MAY BE THERE. YOU THREE TAKE COVER!
FOOSH
!
WAIT, KOTOHA! IT'S TOO DANGER-OUS!
WE'LL TRY TO BRING HIM BACK TO HIS SENSES!

STOP!
BUT I'LL TRY!
I PROMISE I WON'T TURN INTO A DEMON!

I'LL STOP HIM! MY FRIENDS LENS SHOULD CALM HIM DOWN...
I HAVE MY DOUBTS, NASAKE, BUT IT'S WORTH A TRY.
AND I'LL BACK YOU UP!
TWINKLE TWINKLE

MIKUSA!
NASAKE!

I BELIEVE IN HIM.
I'VE GOT TO GO!

TMP
TMP
HE MADE ME A PROMISE!
ARATA WILL COME BACK LIKE HE DID BEFORE.

THERE HE IS!
ARATA!
STOP!
TH
SHEEN
WELL, THEN ...
A WALL OF AIR!
ZEKUU!

HOMURA!
KOOSH
KADOWAKI!
TMP
AGH...

HEH HEH HEH...
ARE YOU IN PAIN?
KADO-WAKI?
...
THE TABLES HAVE TURNED...
HINOHARA IS CHASING ME.
AARGH!
...TRYING TO CATCH UP.
...I WAS ALWAYS BEHIND HIM...
BACK THEN, NO MATTER HOW HARD I TRIED...

UNH...
YOUR BANDAGES AND DRESSINGS NEED CHANGING.
I'LL DO IT RIGHT NOW.
BA-BUMP
UNGH!
...I WAS ALWAYS CHASING HIM.
EVEN AFTER I CAME TO THIS WORLD...
MUNAKATA, WERE YOU WATCHING FROM THE AIRSHIP?
SWUP
I DIDN'T MAKE KANATE SUBMIT.
SWUP
...
HE CHOOSE TO DO IT.
(SWUP)
(SWUP)
WHY?

HE WAS HINO-HARA'S FRIEND, AND YET...
SO FROM NOW ON... HE'S ALL YOURS.
SRK
YOU ALREADY KNOW THE ANSWER TO THAT.
I ONLY BROUGHT HIM ALONG BECAUSE I THOUGHT HE COULD BE USEFUL.
Ah...
I SEE.
WE WERE'N'T TOGETHER FOR VERY LONG.
THAT'S TRUE.
WE DIDN'T SPEND MUCH TIME TALKING OR ANYTHING.

THERE. THAT SHOULD DO IT.
SRK
STILL...
IT'S NOT A BAD THING TO HAVE.
FRIEND-SHIP, I MEAN.

KANATE!
HE BLEW OUT THE FLAMES!
SHOOM

YATAKA!
THE DEMON POWER HAS US TRAPPED.
AND THE WALL OF AIR!
FW
!
SUCH POWER...
NOT EVEN THE SIX SHO COULD MATCH IT!
MY KAMUI KEEPS GETTING WEAKER.
WOO
SH
SHO ARATA...
MY AMA-TSU-RIKI WON'T WORK!

KOTOHA!
ARATA!
HUFF HUFF
HEY, HINOHARA!

...
IS THIS REALLY...
LOOK, KANATE.
YOU KNOW I'M HERE TO TAKE YOU ON...
HINOHARA! DON'T LET IKISU'S KAMUI FOOL YOU!
...WHAT YOU HAD...
...IN MIND FOR US?

...BUT NOT WHEN YOU'RE LIKE THIS!
BACK OFF! NOW!
YOU FORCED KANATE TO SUBMIT...
BETRAYER!
...

BOOM
ARATA...
STOP!
SNAP OUT OF IT!
TWNP
ARATA!
TWNP

ARATA ...
GET...
...AHOLD OF YOUR-SELF!

!
KOTOHA!

Chapter 206
SHOCK

THUMP
KOTOHA!

AH...
SHAKE
KOTO...
HA...
SHAKE
SHAKE

HINO-HARA ...
KOTOHA!
SHAKE SHAKE
SHAKE SHAKE
HIS DEMON AURA IS SUB-SIDING!

KOTOHA! OH, MY GOD...
CARE-FUL! DON'T TRY TO MOVE HER!
WOOSH
KOTOHA!
SHE'S STILL BREATHING. IT'S ALL RIGHT. SHE JUST FAINTED.
BUT ALL THIS BLOOD!
HERE, LET ME...
SWUMP
ARATA!
HE'S BACK TO NORMAL.
WMM

MUNAKATA! WHAT'S WITH YOU?
...
!
GRR
...
WE SHOULD RETURN TO THE AIRSHIP!

SWSH
OKAY, EASY DOES IT.

NEXT TIME...
...HINO-HARA.

UNH...
HOW DO YOU FEEL, KOTOHA ?
WHERE'S ...
... ARATA ...?
...
CHAK
ARATA?
KOTOHA IS...

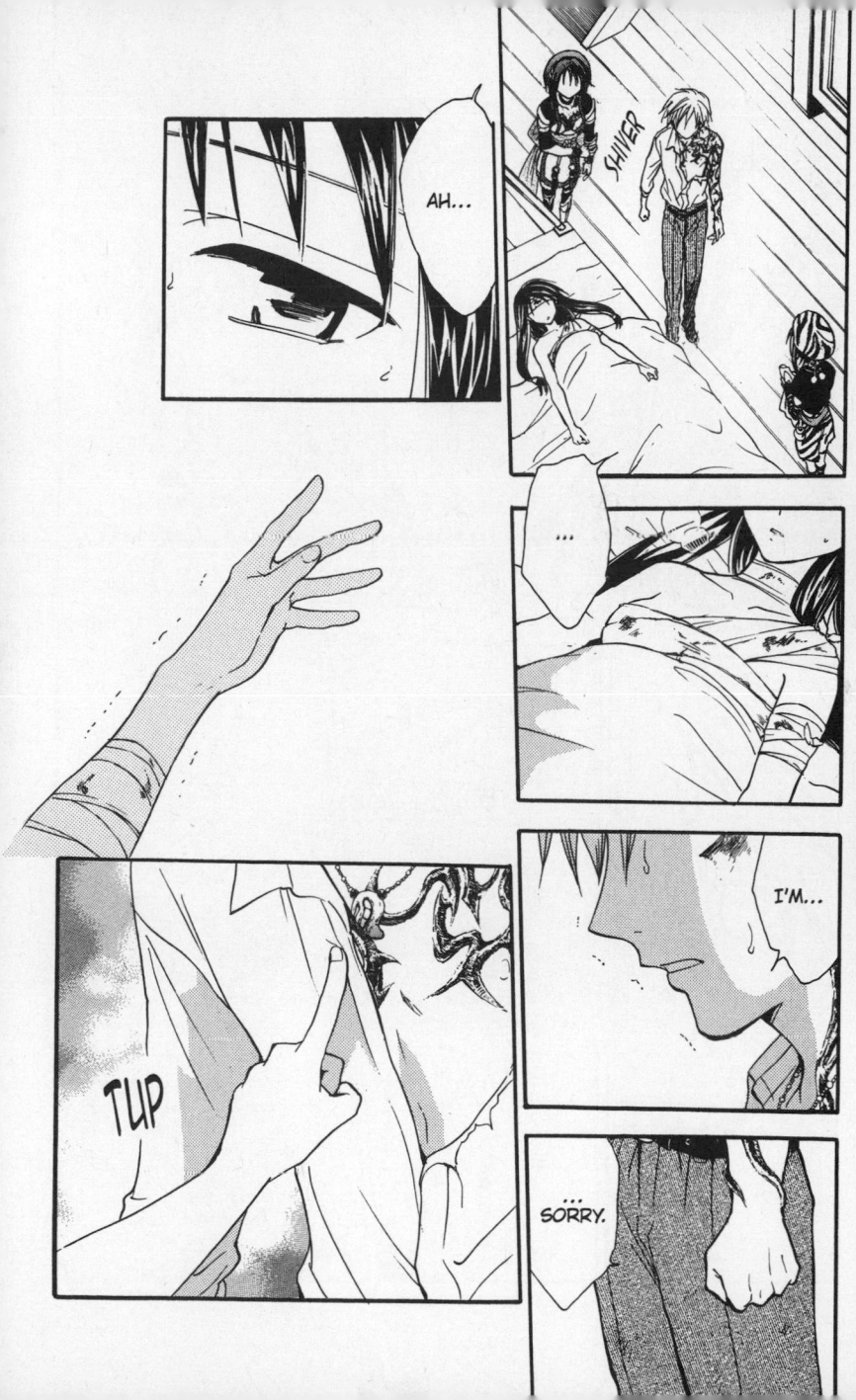
SHIVER
AH...
...
TUP
I'M...
...
SORRY.

Y-
YOU...
...FEEL WORSE...
...THAN I DO.

ARATA ...
KR
CHAK
!

KANATE WAS FORCED TO SUBMIT ...
...BY OROCHI'S SHO?
YES.
I MADE HIM SUBMIT.

SINCE IT GOT DARK THE DEMON AURA...
YATAKA ...
DON'T GO OUTSIDE. IF IKISU SHOULD ATTACK...
ARATA!
...HAS BEEN WEAK-ENING.

BLAST IT!
WHY MUST YOU APPEAR WHEN NIGHT FALLS? AND NOW...
GAH
I'M SCARED. SCARED...
SCARED ...
I'M SCARED OF THE NIGHT.
...WHEN I MIGHT'VE DEFEATED ARATA HINOHARA!
KRK
KRK
I'M GOING TO HIDE.
I'M SCARED ...
I'M SCARED.
LANG
SPLASH

SPLASH
SPLASH
UNH...
SWUSH
ZANG

HELLO, ARATA.
SWFF
...NOT TO NOTICE MY APPROACH.
HOW CARELESS OF YOU...

SEO?
SWO
P
I'VE TRAVELED FAR SINCE LEAVING ISORA'S DOMAIN.
(SIGH)
I THOUGHT I'D CAMP OUT.
EVEN AFTER TRAINING WITH YOU AT AMA-NO-IWAKURA!
I...
...DEMONIZED AGAIN.
DON'T ...DON'T LOOK AT ME!

AND AFTER I PROMISED I'D NEVER TURN INTO A DEMON AGAIN.
I...I DID THIS TO KOTOHA! I BETRAYED HER!
I'M SUCH A JERK! NO, WORSE—A MONSTER.
KANATE ...
MY FRIEND WAS FORCED TO SUBMIT TO KADOWAKI.
AND THAT'S WHY I...
BUT...
I ENDED UP BADLY INJURING KOTOHA...

SWF
IS THAT SO?
HOW HARD IT MUST'VE BEEN.
UNGH...

WHAT'LL I DO? WHAT'LL I DO...IF KOTOHA DIES?
SHE CAN'T USE HER POWERS ON HERSELF!
I SEE. ALL RIGHT...
SEO...!
DON'T WORRY.
WE'LL FIND THE MEANS TO HEAL KOTOHA...
...IN THE CITY!
WE'RE GOING INTO THE CITY, ARATA.
HUH?

Chapter 207
TO THE CITY

SEO!
IS THAT TRUE? IF I TAKE KOTOHA TO THE CITY, I CAN SAVE HER?
YES.
We'll follow this path.
WE NEED TO FIND SOMEONE FROM THE UNEME CLAN...
...WHO HAS THE SAME HEALING POWERS AS KOTOHA.
HUH?
DIDN'T I TELL YOU BEFORE THAT I'VE RUN INTO MEMBERS OF THE HIME CLAN IN EVERY PART OF THE COUNTRY I'VE VISITED?
HIME AND THE UNEME WHO SERVE THEM...
...ARE VERY LIKELY PRESENT IN THE CITY.

RIGHT! AND ANOTHER UNEME...
...WILL BE ABLE TO HEAL KOTOHA'S WOUNDS!
EXACTLY!
SO CHEER UP, ARATA.
SPLASH
KOTOHA ...
HANG IN THERE UNTIL I FIND SOMEONE BELONGING TO YOUR CLAN!
UNH...
BE STRONG, KOTOHA!
THE BLEEDING WON'T STOP...
WE'VE USED EVERY RESOURCE ABOARD THIS SHIP AND NOTHING'S WORKED.

STAY WITH HER, MIKUSA. I'LL BE BACK.
TMP
NASAKE!
...TO FIND A HEALER!
OKAY! I'M GOING TO TOWN...
HAVE YOU FORGOTTEN?
BUT THIS IS IKISU'S DOMAIN!
IT'S TOO DANGEROUS.
YOU KNOW THAT'LL NEVER WORK ON IKISU...
Oh, never mind.
AND I HAVE FRIENDS LENS!
I'M A ZOKUSHO. MY MASTER IS LORD AMEENO, OF THE SIX SHO!
HOLD ON, HOLD ON.
RIGHT! SO I'M GOING.
STILL, WE HAVE TO...
...DO SOMETHING FOR KOTOHA.

I HATE TO SAY WE DON'T TRUST YOU, NASAKE, BUT WE DON'T! GO WITH HIM, KANNAGI.
LORD KANNAGI?
AS YOU POINT OUT, YOU'RE THE ZOKUSHO OF ONE OF THE SIX SHO.

DON'T FORGET IT WAS YOU WHO STRUCK THE BLOW!
...YOU ALMOST KILLED THE WOMAN YOU LOVE. I GUESS YOU KNOW HOW HE FEELS.

I THINK WE SHOULD LEAVE HIM ALONE FOR NOW.
WHAT ABOUT ARATA?
WELL...

WHUP
BECAUSE WE SMELL.
IKISU TAKES AWAY THEIR SCENTS BUT NOT THEIR SENSE OF SMELL.
WHY ARE THEY STARING AT US?
THEY PROBABLY CAN'T EVEN TASTE THEIR FOOD.
THEY ALL LOOK THE SAME.
THERE'S NO LIFE IN THEM.

...
THERE'S ABSOLUTELY NO SCENT HERE.
AN UNEME'S AMATSURIKI WOULD PROBABLY PROTECT HER. IN OTHER WORDS ...
... WE'LL SMELL HER OUT.
SO WE'RE LOOKING FOR SOMEONE... ODOROUS?
YES! HOW'S YOUR NOSE, ARATA?
ARATA ?
SEO...
AREN'T YOU DISAPPOINTED THAT I DEMONIZED?
I FEEL WRETCHED FOR HURTING KOTOHA.
BUT...

I'LL NEVER FORGIVE KADO-WAKI ...
...FOR MAKING MY FRIEND SUBMIT!

I'M GOING TO GET KANATE BACK...
...AND TO DO THAT I SWEAR...
...TO MAKE KADO-WAKI SUBMIT!
WE'LL NEVER BE FRIENDS AGAIN! WHY DID I EVER THINK WE WOULD?
I TRIED TO BELIEVE IN HIM...
...BUT HE BE-TRAYED ME EVERY TIME!
BY FORCE?
I CAN'T CHANGE HOW KADOWAKI FEELS ABOUT ME!
I SEE.
IT'S ALL RIGHT IF YOU FEEL THAT WAY NOW.

AS LONG AS YOU TAKE RESPON-SIBILITY...
...FOR YOUR FEELINGS AND ACTIONS.
PERSONAL RESPON-SIBILITY.

BA-BUMP
SEO?
HUH?
BA-BUMP
KADO-WAKI'S TO BLAME!
NO WAY!
BA-BUMP
FOR KANATE, FOR KOTOHA... FOR EVERY-THING!
BA-BUMP
BA-BUMP
DID I SAY...
...SOMETHING WRONG?
BA-BUMP

SEO...
WHUP
AH!
!

WOO
TMP
WHAT WAS THAT?
THAT'S...
...AN AIRSHIP OF...
...ONE OF THE SIX SHO!

LORD AMEENO!
HEH...
YOUR GUARD IS DOWN, IKISU.

SHUDDER
SHUDDER
I'M SCARED.
SCARED ...
!
OWT
OWT

WHUP
MY CITY!

ANNIHILATE THE INHABITANTS.
DESTROY.
WOOO
AND THE STINK OF... AMEENO!

WHAT'S GOING ON? WHO'S ATTACKING?
AAA
H
SEEMS THERE'S A FALLING OUT AMONG THE SIX SHO...
HUH? NO WAY!

ARATA!
KOTOHA!
WE MUST HURRY AND FIND WHAT WE'VE COME FOR.

BY ASSISTANT

KANNAGI'S ...55... Hayagami Collection PART 3

KANNAGI'S
YATAKA'S
HAYAGAMI COLLECTION
I'LL TAKE OVER NOW.
HE DOESN'T KNOW ANY-THING.
SUKU-NA
THIS IS THE HAYAGAMI OF ZOKUSHO KABANE.
LENGTH: 25 CM. IT CAN EVEN SHRINK AND BECOME A MICRO-SWORD. IT HAS MEDICINAL POWERS, BUT IF OVERUSED CAN BECOME TOXIC.
IT'S A FLOWER.
SAKU-YA
THIS IS THE HAYAGAMI OF ZOKUSHO OCHIRU.
LENGTH: ONE METER. IT'S SHAPED LIKE A FLOWER AND SYMBOLIZES LIFE.
IT TURNS INTO A HUGE BLOSSOM AND ITS LIFE FORCE CAN BE SHARED WITH HUMANS. THIS HAYAGAMI GAVE ME AN AWFUL TIME.
TAJI-KARA
THIS HAYAGAMI BELONGS TO SARUTA.
THIS IS THE HAYAGAMI THAT CAME TO MY RESCUE AT AMA-NO-IWAKURA.
LENGTH: 10 M. IT SYMBOLIZES THE POWER OF THE UNIVERSE. ITS KAMUI CONTROLS MOVE-MENT. IF IT WERE LOST, THE WORLD WOULD STOP ROTATING.
BALL
Four cog wheels
SHOOM KLANK
That's the sound it makes.
NO-ZUCHI
THIS IS THE HAYAGAMI OF ZOKUSHO KABANE.
LENGTH: 40 CM. IT CONTROLS PLANTS. AKACHI LONG WISHED TO HAVE THIS HAYAGAMI IN HIS TERRITORY, HANIYASU. IF ONLY HE'D HAD IT 150 YEARS AGO...
It's about this big.
THE END

I took my family to an *onsen* hot spring in Shuzenji. We all need a break sometimes! As well as family time!

...I had nothing pending during the week I reserved the rooms for. (Or so I thought.) I worked up until the day we were to leave! Oh no, will I make it?! Uh-oh (°д°;), I nearly panicked! We somehow managed to go on our trip, and it was divine. The hot spring was amazing. The food was delicious. But upon returning home, I was faced with deadlines again! The negatives made the plusses turn to zero. But it became an even bigger – (minus). I just wasn't feeling physically well. Long story short, I collapsed and landed in the hospital. Don't put up with it until it's too late! I've never had so many IVs in my life!

I'm usually quite healthy.

Even my chiropractor says, "You have a sturdy body."

...There's nothing scarier when your stamina goes!

It's a stretch to keep my body in good health!

I'll do something about it before the next volume!

–Yuu Watase

AUTHOR BIO

Born March 5 in Osaka, Yuu Watase debuted in the *Shôjo Comic* manga anthology in 1989. She won the 43rd Shogakukan Manga Award with *Ceres: Celestial Legend*. One of her most famous works is *Fushigi Yûgi*, a series that has inspired the prequel *Fushigi Yûgi: Genbu Kaiden*. In 2008, *Arata: The Legend* started serialization in *Shonen Sunday*.

LV
MAY 26, 2015

ARATA: THE LEGEND
Volume 21
Shonen Sunday Edition

Story and Art by YUU WATASE

ARATA KANGATARI Vol. 21
by Yuu WATASE
© 2009 Yuu WATASE
All rights reserved.
Original Japanese edition p
English translation rights i
Kingdom and Ireland arran

English Adaptation: Lance Caselman
Translation: JN Productions
Touch-up Art & Lettering: Rina Mapa
Design: Veronica Casson
Editor: Gary Leach

The stories, characters and incidents mentioned in this publication are entirely fictional.

No portion of this book may be reproduced or transmitted in any form or by any means without written permission from the copyright holders.

Printed in the U.S.A.

Published by VIZ Media, LLC
P.O. Box 77010
San Francisco, CA 94107

10 9 8 7 6 5 4 3 2 1
First printing, March 2015

www.viz.com

WWW.SHONENSUNDAY.COM